WILD AND WACKY INVENTIONS

WEIRD FOOD INVENTIONS

BY JILL KEPPELER

Gareth Stevens PUBLISHING

Please visit our website, www.garethstevens.com. For a free color catalog of all our high-quality books, call toll free 1-800-542-2595 or fax 1-877-542-2596.

Cataloging-in-Publication Data

Names: Keppeler, Jill.
Title: Weird food inventions / Jill Keppeler.
Description: New York : Gareth Stevens Publishing, 2019. | Series: Wild and wacky inventions | Includes glossary and index.
Identifiers: LCCN ISBN 9781538220733 (pbk.) | ISBN 9781538220719 (library bound) | ISBN 9781538220740 (6 pack)
Subjects: LCSH: Food–History–Juvenile literature. | Inventions–History–Juvenile literature.
Classification: LCC TX355.K47 2019 | DDC 641.309–dc23

First Edition

Published in 2019 by
Gareth Stevens Publishing
111 East 14th Street, Suite 349
New York, NY 10003

Designer: Sarah Liddell
Editor: Kate Mikoley

Photo credits: Cover, background throughout book ninjaudom/Shutterstock.com; cover, p. 1 (spaghetti fork) Evans/Hulton Archive/Getty Images; cover, p. 1 (hand mixer used throughout book) lynea/Shutterstock.com; cover, p. 1 (garlic crusher) MiaMilky/Shutterstock.com; pp. 5, 7, 9, 11, 13, 15, 17, 19, 21, 23, 25, 27, 29 (hand used throughout) Helena Ohman/Shutterstock.com; pp. 5, 7, 9, 11, 13, 15, 17, 19, 21, 23, 25, 27, 29 (texture throughout) Alex Gontar/Shutterstock.com; p. 5 Bloomberg/Contributor/Bloomberg/Getty Images; p. 7 (spork) Lori Werhane/Shutterstock.com; p. 7 (splayd) Flickr upload bot/Wikimedia Commons; p. 9 Fæ/Wikimedia Commons; p. 11 Evans/Stringer/Hulton Archive/Getty Images; p. 13 SportSuburban/Flickr; p. 15 54613/Shutterstock.com; p. 17 AFP/Contributor/AFP/Getty Images; p. 19 Akron Beacon Journal/Contributor/Tribune News Service/Getty Images; p. 21 Rae Russel/Contributor/Archive Photos/Getty Images; p. 23 Mircea Costina/Shutterstock.com; p. 27 Barcroft/Contributor/Barcroft Media/Getty Images; p. 29 Charoenkrung.Studio99/Shutterstock.com.

Printed in the United States of America

CPSIA compliance information: Batch #CS18GS: For further information contact Gareth Stevens, New York, New York at 1-800-542-2595.

CONTENTS

Fun with Food 4
The Story of the Spork 6
Unusual Utensils 8
The Wily Wizard 10
Absurd Appliances 12
Egg-citing! 14
Such Strange Shapes 16
Print It, Eat It 18
Vending It All 20
The Terror of the Dinner Party 22
Spam I Am 24
Fried Everything 26
Into the Weird Future 28
Glossary 30
For More Information 31
Index 32

Words in the glossary appear in **bold** type the first time they are used in the text.

FUN WITH FOOD

Every human on the planet has this in common: We all need to eat! From something as simple as a banana to as complicated as the fanciest wedding cake, we eat lots of different things. And people keep coming up with new foods to eat and new ways to eat them.

Inventions have been very important to the history of food. Without refrigeration, people couldn't preserve foods to eat later. Without ovens or stoves, we couldn't cook meat. And without mills of various kinds, we wouldn't be able to make flour and thus bread—or cake or cookies!

But for every invention that changes the way we eat forever, there are dozens that don't work out quite as well. You might even say that they're, well, weird!

WACKY WONDERS

One popular treat definitely wouldn't exist without the refrigerator: the Popsicle! Eleven-year-old Frank Epperson invented this frozen treat in 1905.

REFRIGERATORS TODAY ARE A LOT FANCIER THAN THEY WERE WHEN FIRST INVENTED! SOME REFRIGERATORS TODAY CAN EVEN CONNECT TO THE INTERNET!

MAKING FOOD COOL

In 2012, the Royal Society of the United Kingdom came up with a list of the 20 most important inventions in the history of food and drink. Refrigeration was at the top of the list. People first invented **artificial** refrigerators in the mid-1700s and first produced them for sale in 1805. There were also much older inventions on the list, including the fishing net and the plow. People have used these things since the Stone Age!

THE STORY OF THE SPORK

People use different utensils, or tools, to eat their food. These may vary from place to place. Sometimes inventors decide we need new ways to eat, however, and the results can be pretty wacky!

One tale about the invention of the spork involves Douglas MacArthur, a US general who was stationed in Japan in the 1940s after World War II. The story says that MacArthur thought prisoners might use forks to attack guards and escape, so he invented the spork.

This story is just a legend, however. People used the spork well before this. A man named Samuel W. Francis first patented the idea in 1874. Francis was quite an inventor. He also created a typewriter that looked like a piano and a self-opening **coffin**.

WACKY WONDERS

A spork is a combination spoon and fork. It has a bowl like a spoon, but **tines** like a fork. The word first appeared in 1909, and people still use sporks today, but they don't really work very well.

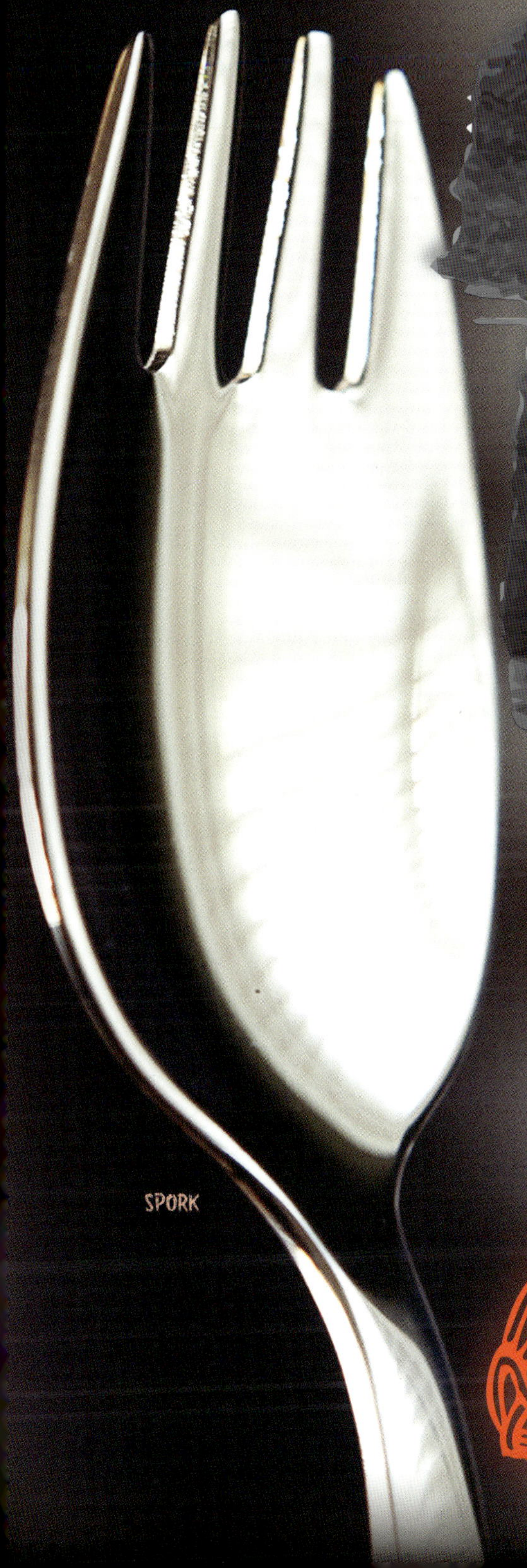

SPORK

BY ANY OTHER NAME

Sporks aren't the only weird combination utensil out there. Australian William MacArthur (no relation to Douglas MacArthur) created the "Splayd" in 1943. This utensil is a combination spoon, fork, and knife. It's still popular in Australia, where people have purchased more than 5 million of the tools. Inventors have also created "knorks" (a fork with a cutting edge), "spifes" (a spoon with a handle that can cut fruit), and "chorks" (a combination of a fork and **chopsticks**).

SPLAYD

A US COMPANY REGISTERED A TRADEMARK FOR THE NAME "SPORK" IN 1970. THIS MEANS IT HAD THE RIGHT TO USE THE NAME TO SELL ITS PRODUCTS.

UNUSUAL UTENSILS

The world of unusual utensils doesn't end with sporks. Inventors continued creating new ways to eat. You can find **tongs**, spoons, or toothpicks that fit over your fingers, or caps that fit on pens to work like spoons, forks, or knives!

Some of these tools seem like they might be useful (such as a knife that heats up so it's easier to spread cold butter), but some might make you wonder if it would be less work to just use an ordinary spoon or knife—or even your hands. Do we really need a hooklike tool that people can use to dip cookies in milk or a toy gun that you can use to "shoot" ketchup or mustard onto a hot dog? Someone thought so!

WACKY WONDERS

When canned foods hit the market in the United States, people who'd never eaten seafood could finally try it! Canned sardines were very popular, and people created a weird new fork just to get them out of the container.

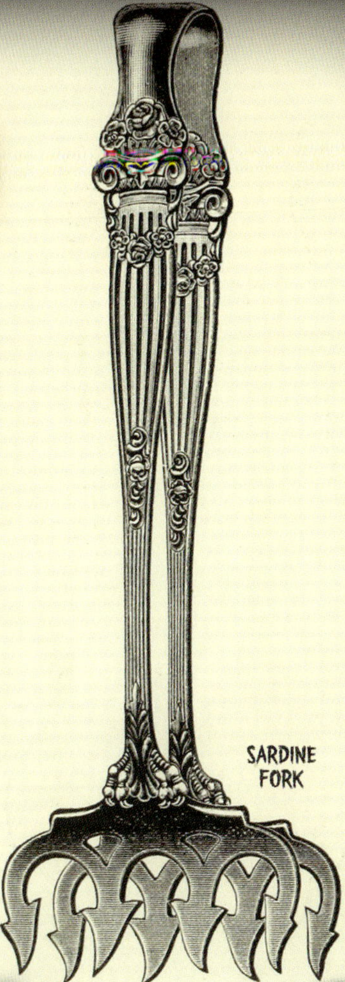

SARDINE FORK

BONBON SPOON

TIMES CHANGE

Many weird food utensils are relatively recent inventions, but some older tools seem pretty unusual today, too. There were usually reasons for them, however. Fruit pocketknives sound odd, but men would carry them just to show they had the money to buy fresh fruit in the days before cheap cross-country shipping. And in the 1880s, people used bonbon spoons for chocolates because the treat could be very sticky and messy in the time before refrigeration and preservation were common.

THE WILY WIZARD

In the mid-1900s, a man named Russell Oakes became known for creating wacky inventions. Oakes worked in advertising, but he spent his spare time creating goofy devices. Many of these had to do with food. Oakes lived in Waukesha, Wisconsin, but became known around the country. He often showed off his silly inventions and became known to many as the "Wily Wizard of Waukesha."

One of Oakes's inventions was a dripless doughnut dunker that could help people dunk their doughnuts in coffee without spilling any of the liquid. It also prevented those using it from burning themselves on the hot coffee. A special arm dunked the doughnut into the coffee, and a small pan would help raise the doughnut to the person's mouth.

WACKY WONDERS

Another one of Oakes's inventions was a self-winding fork that could twirl spaghetti without the person using it having to turn the fork on their own!

OAKES DID MOST OF HIS INVENTING IN HIS BASEMENT. HE CAME UP WITH MORE THAN 50 INVENTIONS, MANY OF WHICH COULD BE USED IN THE KITCHEN!

A CELEBRITY OF SORTS

Oakes was as much an entertainer as he was an inventor. Most of his inventions weren't very practical, but they made people laugh! In 1935, he started showing some of his inventions at local meetings and events around Wisconsin. It wasn't long before people across the country knew who Oakes was. He was featured, along with his inventions, in a number of short films and national television shows.

ABSURD APPLIANCES

An appliance is a piece of equipment designed for a specific use. Today, there are many common large kitchen appliances, such as stoves and refrigerators. But just like utensils, sometimes people create appliances that can be a bit strange. And just like with utensils, some of the oddest tend to combine two or more things into one.

An advertisement from the General Air Conditioning Corporation back in the 1950s shows a combination stove-refrigerator-sink designed for small spaces, which would at least be practical. Other combination appliances went in the opposite direction. An ad from 1955 shows a General Electric "Wonder Kitchen" that's 9.5 feet (2.9 m) long and includes a dishwasher, sink, stove, washing machine (for clothes), and dryer. Buyers could also add a refrigerator!

WACKY WONDERS

In 1885, a woman named Agnes Marshall invented an ice cream maker that could create the sweet treat in less than 5 minutes. But there was one big problem: The device was made of zinc, making the finished ice cream toxic!

FAST FOOD?

Over the years, inventors have also tried to combine the machines we use to cook and the ones we use to travel. Back in the 1910s, when automobiles were still new, inventor R. L. Martin created a gadget that turned a car into a kitchen on the move, although apparently it didn't catch on. People have also invented devices that allowed them to cook burgers through their car exhaust system and vehicles that can make coffee!

EGG-CITING!

Humans have been eating eggs about as long as we've been on this planet. So, it's not really surprising that we've come up with all sorts of creative ways to cook them. It goes beyond the usual boiled, scrambled, or fried question: There are gadgets that will let you cook eggs in strange shapes such as cubes or tubes—or even in the shape of a heart or a skull!

It's pretty easy to cook eggs to begin with, but some people try to make it even easier. In 2015, one company started selling a preboiled egg. All you had to do was add boiling water! (Although that's really how you boil eggs anyway.) There's also a tool that lets people scramble their eggs before they even crack the shell. Weird!

WACKY WONDERS

As **technology** changes, inventions change, too. You can buy an egg tray that connects to a smartphone app to let you know how many eggs you have in your fridge and how old they are.

FAST FOOD?

Egg gadgets have been around for a long time. There are special tools to hold boiling eggs and time how long they've been cooking, pans to poach eggs in, devices to separate egg whites from their **yolks**, and even gadgets with which to slice eggs. Some inventions were meant to keep cooked eggs from cooling. In the days when servants in bigger households carried meals from the kitchen to the dining room, people often used special containers to keep breakfast eggs warm.

POACHING AN EGG MEANS TO COOK IT IN A LIQUID THAT'S JUST UNDER THE BOILING POINT. EGGS CAN ALSO BE BOILED, FRIED, OR BAKED.

SUCH STRANGE SHAPES

Cube-shaped eggs sound pretty weird, but that's not the only food people try to cook in odd shapes. It's common for cooks to try to make foods look like other foods—or not like foods at all! There are molds that let you make cakes, chocolates, or other treats into the shape of movie characters, cars, teddy bears, dinosaurs—or even poop. Yuck!

People have also invented gadgets that let nature itself shape foods such as apples and watermelons. A Chinese company called Fruit Mould sells plastic molds that let gardeners shape still-growing fruits and vegetables. You can have heart-shaped apples, skull-shaped pumpkins, or star-shaped cucumbers! You just need to put the mold on the fruit or vegetable when it's still very small.

WACKY WONDERS

The Japanese practice of mukimono involves carving fruits and vegetables into beautiful works of art. You can buy special sets of knives and tools for this art.

EDIBLE ART

Artists have used special molds, tools, and skill to make **edible** works of art for thousands of years. Back in 18th-century Europe, an artist might have made a fancy sugar palace as a centerpiece for a wedding celebration. Cooks also made decorations out of **pastry** or bread for important dinners during **medieval** times. These fancy works were called subtleties. Sometimes they were edible, sometimes they weren't! They were entertainment even more than they were food.

PRINT IT, EAT IT

Today, people aren't limited to molds for weird-shaped foods. Would you like to eat a pancake shaped like your favorite comic character? What about a pancake shaped like a rocket ship? Using 3-D printing technology, the PancakeBot lets you make breakfast treats shaped like anything! Miguel Valenzuela, an inventor from Norway, first created the gadget for his daughters using LEGO blocks. It went on sale in 2016.

Don't want to be limited to pancakes? Students at the Massachusetts Institute of Technology came up with the Cornucopia, a 3-D printer that prints food using fresh ingredients. Others have created printers that focus on pizza, pasta, or candy. It sounds fun, but there's a practical reason for it, too. Printers could reduce kitchen waste or add **vitamins** to make food healthier.

WACKY WONDERS

Dylan's Candy Bar in New York City sells 3-D printed gummy candy. You can pick the shape, the color, and the flavor of your treat!

THE PANCAKEBOT WAS SHOWN OFF IN 2016 AT THE INTERNATIONAL HOME AND HOUSEWARES SHOW IN CHICAGO, ILLINOIS.

FOOD OF THE FUTURE?

In 2017, a pair of professors at the Hebrew University of Jerusalem presented a 3-D printer that uses a material called nanocellulose to print food. It doesn't sound tasty—nanocellulose is a plastic-like material that's made from plants and is stronger than steel—but people can control the taste, feel, and **nutritional value** of the final product, as well as how it's cooked.

VENDING IT ALL

Vending machines have been around for decades, but today inventors around the world have taken them beyond potato chips and chocolate bars to items such as caviar (fish eggs) and hot dogs.

Cupcake bakery Sprinkles stocks "cupcake ATMs" with fresh treats in about 15 locations throughout the United States. The machine doesn't bake the cupcakes, but it's stocked throughout the day by bakery employees. When someone buys a cupcake, a robotic arm inside the ATM selects their treat from within its stock and deposits it in a small box, which then is placed in a revolving door below.

People in Japan are particularly fond of vending machines. There, you can find ones that dispense fish soup, noodles, eggs, rice, hamburgers, freshly made popcorn, bread in a can, and a lot more!

WACKY WONDERS

A restaurant in Las Vegas, Nevada, used to have a lobster vending machine. To get your lobster, you had to first catch it with a mechanical claw that dipped into a tank full of live lobsters!

ONE OF THE REASONS THE AUTOMATS CLOSED WAS THAT RISING PRICES MADE THEIR COIN-OPERATED PLAN IMPOSSIBLE. VENDING MACHINES SUCH AS THE CUPCAKE ATM MAKE IT POSSIBLE FOR CUSTOMERS TO USE TOUCHSCREENS AND DIGITAL PAYMENTS.

THE AUTOMAT

During the middle of the 20th century, many cities in the United States had Automats, which were cafeterias in which all of the food came from vending machines. The Horn & Hardart Company operated many of the restaurants, which contained walls full of windowed boxes, each with a food item such as a slice of pie or a sandwich. Customers put coins into slots in the boxes to get their food while workers behind the scenes refilled the boxes.

THE TERROR OF THE DINNER PARTY

Sometimes people invent things that have to do with eating, creating, or selling food—but sometimes they invent the foods themselves! There have been many weird food creations of this sort throughout history, and some of them sound pretty terrible to us today. Starting during the early 20th century, many cooks created gelatin salads, which featured all kinds of ingredients submerged in sweet, colorful flavored gelatin and poured into a mold.

This might sound good—but those ingredients could include things from canned pears and marshmallows to chopped cabbage, olives, pickles, hard-boiled eggs, chicken, tomatoes, tuna, and other not-so-sweet ingredients. These salads were popular for a long time, but they began to fall out of favor in the 1970s and 1980s. Aren't you glad?

WACKY WONDERS

One old advertisement for Jell-O features a recipe for a salad that includes lime Jell-O, onion, cottage cheese, mayonnaise, and seafood salad. Would you try it?

THE HISTORY BEHIND THE HORROR

There are historical reasons why gelatin salads became popular when they did. Dishes that used gelatin go back a long time, but they were expensive and hard to make. Jell-O—an inexpensive, fruit-flavored gelatin—first became widely available at the beginning of the 1900s, right around the same time as home refrigerators. It could be made fast and gave foods a neat appearance. Gelatin salads looked fancy but didn't cost a lot, so people tried them with every ingredient possible!

SPAM I AM

Canned food is pretty boring, right? Well, back when it first became common, people thought it was quite exciting! Canning let people eat foods such as meats and vegetables even when fresh ones weren't available. It also led to new food inventions that took advantage of the technology.

In 1937, a man named Jay Hormel was looking for a good way to can the meat his family's business produced. This was tough, because the heat from the canning process would dry the meat out. Hormel hit on a combination of pork, salt, water, sugar, and other ingredients, which was packed in a square can and named "Spam." Square meat may not sound very appetizing, but the Hormel Company has sold more than 8 billion cans over the past 81 years!

WACKY WONDERS

Spam may be a little weird, but it's not the oddest canned food out there. You also can buy canned whole chickens, horse milk, and reindeer and armadillo meat!

WARTIME SPAM

Hormel's canned meat products became very important during World War II. The United States sent more than 100 million cans to the Pacific to serve as meals for soldiers. Because the soldiers ate so much of it, Spam became the subject of many jokes, tales, poems, and even songs. Unfortunately for Hormel, however, the soldiers became so sick of Spam that it also inspired a great deal of hate mail to its inventor!

A TIMELINE OF FOOD INVENTIONS AND TRENDS

- **AD 500 TO 1500:** SUBTLETIES BECOME POPULAR IN MEDIEVAL EUROPE.
- **MID-1700s:** PEOPLE FIRST INVENT ARTIFICIAL REFRIGERATION.
- **1805:** REFRIGERATORS FIRST GO ON SALE.
- **1874:** SAMUEL W. FRANCIS FIRST HAS THE IDEA FOR THE SPORK.
- **1880s:** BONBON SPOONS FOR CHOCOLATES BECOME POPULAR.
- **1885:** AGNES MARSHALL INVENTS HER ICE CREAM MAKER.
- **1905:** 11-YEAR-OLD FRANK EPPERSON INVENTS THE POPSICLE.
- **1910s:** R. L. MARTIN INVENTS A KITCHEN FOR YOUR CAR.
- **1912:** THE FIRST AUTOMAT OPENS IN NEW YORK CITY.
- **1937:** JAY HORMEL INVENTS SPAM.
- **1943:** WILLIAM MACARTHUR INVENTS THE SPLAYD.
- **1955:** GENERAL ELECTRIC ADVERTISES THE "WONDER KITCHEN."
- **1991:** THE LAST AUTOMAT IN THE UNITED STATES CLOSES IN MANHATTAN, NEW YORK.
- **2012:** SPRINKLES OPENS ITS FIRST CUPCAKE ATM IN BEVERLY HILLS, CALIFORNIA.
- **2016:** MIGUEL VALENZUELA STARTS SELLING THE PANCAKEBOT.
- **2017:** PROFESSORS AT THE HEBREW UNIVERSITY OF JERUSALEM PRESENT A 3-D PRINTER THAT USES NANOCELLULOSE.

FRIED EVERYTHING

Of course, weird food inventions aren't just a thing of the past. Today, one popular trend revolves around many county and state fairs across the United States—where you can find almost any food at all dipped in batter and deep-fried! In the late 1990s and early 2000s, cooks at state fairs (especially in Texas) started experimenting and things promptly got a little out of control.

People have now managed to fry bubble gum, Coca-Cola, sticks of butter, birthday cake, Oreo cookies, many kinds of candy bars, sugar cubes, alligator meat, pork chops, lemonade, Twinkies, Kool-Aid, jelly beans, and whole hamburgers—complete with bun. Cooks have even stuffed salad in a wrap and then deep-fried that, too. No food is safe from the fryer!

WACKY WONDERS

Fried foods have been around for centuries. The Egyptians first deep-fried foods back around 5000 BC.

FRIED FOOD TASTES GOOD BECAUSE OF THE MAILLARD REACTION. THIS REACTION BETWEEN SUGARS AND PROTEINS HAPPENS WHEN SOME FOODS ARE HEATED.

DEEP IN THE HEART OF TEXAS

The State Fair of Texas is fried food central. Every year since 2005, the event has hosted the Big Tex Choice Awards for fair treats. In 2017, judges had to pick from nearly 50 choices, many of them deep-fried. The contest finalists included deep-fried chicken noodle soup on a stick, fried Texas sheet cake, and deep-fried Froot Loops cereal. Cook Abel Gonzales Jr. invented both deep-fried Coca-Cola and deep-fried butter for the contest back in 2006 and 2009.

INTO THE WEIRD FUTURE

As time marches on and we move into the future, we'll probably see even more weird food inventions. As the population grows and more people look for ways to live in a more sustainable manner, we may wind up consuming more unusual things—such as bugs. Or we might eat meat grown in a laboratory and not on a farm.

Meanwhile, it's likely that our kitchens will hold more appliances linked to the web of information around us. There are already apps that connect to our refrigerators and other kitchen items, such as cooking pans, to provide information on what we need to buy at the grocery store or what we've already added to that night's dinner.

There's really no doubt about it—the future of food will be weird.

WACKY WONDERS

Laboratory-grown meat involves taking cells from a real animal and then growing the tissue in a lab. It's a difficult and expensive process, and scientists are still working on it.

MMMM, BUGS!

Eating bugs might sound really weird, but these creepy, crawly critters can be very good for you. They have lots of vitamins, minerals, and protein. And raising bugs takes a lot less food and water than raising cattle: about 10 times less food and 1,500 times less water, according to the United Nations Food and Agriculture Organization. They produce fewer greenhouse gases, too! Crickets, spiders, and mealworms might be on your plate in the future.

IN THIS PHOTO, A CHILD EATS A CHOCOLATE BAR CONTAINING NUTS—AND FRIED INSECTS! WOULD YOU TRY THAT?

GLOSSARY

artificial: made by people and not by nature

chopsticks: a pair of thin sticks held between the thumb and fingers and used to eat

coffin: a box for burying a dead body

edible: able to be eaten

medieval: having to do with the Middle Ages, a time in European history from about AD 500 to AD 1500

nutritional value: the makeup of a food and its impact on the body

pastry: a mix of flour, water, and fat used for desserts such as pies

technology: tools, machines, or ways to do things that use the latest discoveries to fix problems or meet needs

tine: a thin, pointed part of something that sticks out

tongs: a tool with two arms used to hold or pick up things

vend: sell

vitamin: a substance important in small quantities for the nutrition of animals

yolk: the yellow part in the center of an egg

FOR MORE INFORMATION

BOOKS

Bader, Bonnie. *Curious About Ice Cream*. New York, NY: Penguin Young Readers Licenses, 2017.

Higgins, Nadia. *Fun Food Inventions*. Minneapolis, MN: Lerner Publications, 2014.

Kurlansky, Mark. *Frozen in Time: Clarence Birdseye's Outrageous Idea About Frozen Food*. New York, NY: Delacorte Press, 2014.

WEBSITES

Crazy Kids' Inventions Turned Into Real Products
boredpanda.com/kids-inventions-turned-into-reality-inventors-project-dominic-wilcox/
Kids can be inventors, too! See some products that were invented by children just like you.

Food History
delish.com/food/g1979/food-history/
Learn weird facts about your favorite foods and appliances!

Inventors—How to Become an Inventor
easyscienceforkids.com/all-about-inventors/
Learn how to become an inventor yourself!

INDEX

automat 21, 25
bonbon spoon 9, 25
chork 7
Dylan's Candy Bar 18
Epperson, Frank 4, 25
Francis, Samuel W. 6, 25
Fruit Mould 16
General Air Conditioning Corporation 12
General Electric 12
Gonzales, Abel, Jr. 27
Hormel Company 24
Hormel, Jay 24, 25
Horn & Hardart Company 21
Jell-O 22, 23
knork 7
MacArthur, Douglas 6
MacArthur, William 7
Maillard reaction 27
Marshall, Agnes 14, 29
Martin, R. L. 12, 25
mukimono 16
nanocellulose 19, 25
Oakes, Russell 10
PancakeBot 18, 19
Popsicle 4, 25
refrigerators 5, 25
Royal Society of the United Kingdom 5
sardine fork 9
Spam 24, 25
spife 7
splayd 7
spork 6
Sprinkles 20, 25
subtleties 17, 25
3-D printer 18
tongs 8
Valenzuela, Miguel 18, 25
vending machine 20
Wonder Kitchen 12, 13, 25